S0-BAF-467

1

Copyright © 2018 by Kathy Wilson

ALL RIGHTS RESERVED. No part of this book may be reproduced or transmitted in any form or by any means, electronic or mechanical, including photocopying, recording, or by any information storage and retrieval systems without permission of the author except where permitted by law.

Table of Contents

Introduction

Inevitably there will come a point in your life where you'll find yourself stuck, slowed down, or even completely stopped from moving forward with your plans. There are lots of impediments that can stop you from moving toward your goals. Resistance, sabotage (yours and other people's), and energy leaks are just a few items on the extensive list of obstacles that can stop your progress dead in its tracks. During your life you'll no doubt find several more that can be added to the list.

All of these progress blockers have one thing in common. They're all different faces of the same thing. **FEAR.**

Fear is tricky, slippery, and a master of disguises. This makes it exceedingly difficult to recognize that what you're feeling is actually fear. It can appear as one of its more obvious symptoms, such as sweaty palms, heart palpitations, and legs of Jell-O. It can also appear in one of its trickier disguises, such as a sudden desire to organize your desk instead of making phone calls to create new business.

In this book you'll...

- identify how fear shows its many faces to you so that when it does materialize, you'll be able to easily identify it. It's much easier to deal with a challenge when you can recognize it.

- learn how fear affects you mentally and physically.

- explore your fears, learn how to tame them, and turn them into your allies.

By the time you reach the end of this book, you'll have a comfortable working knowledge of your fears and how to use them to your best advantage.

You may wish to have a pen and a notebook handy as you progress through this book so you can record your revelations, discoveries, answers, and solutions that arise as you work through the exercises.

A Brief History of Fear

In the past, fear has proven to be very important, on a personal level as well as collectively as a species. It's *still* very important or it wouldn't be around today.

In the beginning of human evolution, fear was needed for survival. When our Neanderthal ancestors felt fear, they knew instantly that it was time to either run for their lives or fight whatever was threatening them.

Today it serves that same purpose of alerting you to dangers and, thus, insuring your survival. However, there is a major difference in today's world, in that fear now appears in more subtle forms than monster-size dinosaurs. In fact, the object of fear in current times is very often invisible and can appear as failure, rejection, abandonment and other such intangible issues.

Not being able to see the object of your fear makes fighting it much more difficult than the simple chore our ancestors had. They simply bopped the object of their fear - a dinosaur - over the head with their club.

This is Your Brain

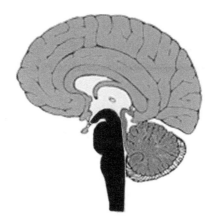

This is Your Brain on Fear

There is a part of your brain that exists solely for your physical survival. It's called the "Reptilian" brain because it's been with us for about 100,000,000 years, since the era of the big reptiles - the dinosaurs. This is the first and only part of the human brain our species had for millions of years.

The main purpose of this original part of the brain was to protect the physical body from harm, thus continuing the survival of the human species. To this day, it serves the same purpose.

As humans evolved, other parts of the brain were formed, such as the limbic system which deals with emotions, and the cerebral portion which is the logical thinking and reasoning part.

The Reptilian part of your brain is located at the stem of the brain, securely cushioned and protected from injury by the rest of the brain. In the event of a major injury to your brain, all the other parts of it may stop functioning, but because this part is so well protected it will probably still be ticking along. This is a very clever and important bit of evolution. You can live without logic and reason. You can live without emotions. But you can't live without your physical body.

The Reptilian brain is command control for your survival instinct, commonly known as the Fight or Flight response. During a state of fear, your physiology changes, and your blood is re-routed to that which you need for survival – muscles, heart, lungs, adrenal glands... and your Reptilian brain.

When you're in fear, *all* conscious brain activity goes to your Reptilian brain while the activity in the remainder of your brain (the thinking and feeling parts) shuts down.

When you're in the emotional state of fear and the Reptilian portion of your brain is in control, you have *only* two choices - either fighting the fearsome thing or running from it. Everything you do will be some form of one of those two choices. Everything.

If you're thinking, "Hoo hah! We're waaay too advanced for that Fight or Flight stuff," just remember the last time you were in a very disagreeable situation.

Perhaps you had a run-in with your boss. Did you want to have a nice cozy, chat with her and work with her to create a viable solution to your common problem? Not likely.

Probably you wanted either to get away and escape her nastiness *or* tell her off. These are Flight and Fight reactions.

When you're experiencing fear you have no capability for creative or even rational thought. It's all fight or flight, good or bad, me or you, right or wrong.

When you're in this state you simply don't have the physiological ability to think of creative, alternative solutions for a win-win solution. Your mental capacity is limited to *only* two choices - Fight or Flight.

How Fear Stops You

As you're hopping and skipping along in your life, you'll come up against many challenges that will induce fear within you, which you will experience to varying degrees. When this happens, your focus will *instantly* revert to survival as the Reptilian brain moves into action, enabling you to see only two solutions: fighting the fearsome object or running away from it.

You'll not be in the mental state for focusing on forward progress, and certainly not for creative solutions to the issue or challenge.

Success? Win-win solutions? How could you *possibly* think of them when you're so busy focusing on fighting your fear or running from it?

Don't fret. There are easy and simple solutions.

A Choiceful State of Being

Julia Cameron in her world-famous book *The Artist's Way* writes about, and for, blocked creatives. That describes not just the writers and artists for whom she initially intended her book, but all of us at one time or another. As you're moving along each day, you're creating your life... and creativity doesn't get much bigger than that.

Being blocked is a fearful state of being.

What keeps you blocked and unable to find creative solutions to your challenges is being in a fearful state. It's like a Catch 22. You can't find solutions to your problems because your problems keep you in a state of fear where you can't find solutions to your problems.

When you're in this state, you're bouncing back and forth between the only two options available to you when your conscious awareness is in your Reptilian brain - the two extremely limiting choices of either flight or fight.

Luckily, our brains evolved and you now have additional portions of your brain which you can utilize.

The cerebral cortex is one of these "new" areas. It's where you think logically and with reason, visualize, and dream. This part of your brain has the capacity to find new opportunities as you "see" the array of choices and solutions available to you.

**Using your cerebral brain
puts you in a choiceful state of being.**

When you move your awareness out of the Reptilian part of your brain and into the cerebral cortex you begin to find choices that are *far* better than the limitation of only fight or flight. You begin to recognize choices that lead to creative solutions, such as collaboration, win/win solutions, harmonious relationships, and most importantly... peace.

Sounds great, doesn't it? But when your consciousness is in the limitation of the fear-based Reptilian brain, how do you move it into the creative cerebral cortex?

The solution is quite simple, actually. All you have to do is visualize.

Visualization

When you visualize, you *instantly* move your awareness out of the Reptilian brain and into the cerebral cortex, allowing the creative portion of your brain to activate. *Now* you can begin to see more choices about your situation - choices that create more beneficial solutions for you *and* for all concerned.

Any form of visualization will work. Here are a few suggestions:

- Imagine a scale with numbers from 1 to 10 and rate the intensity of your fear on this scale. As you move your consciousness out of your Reptilian brain by visualizing the scale, what choices do you now begin to see that will move your fear down a few notches?

- Close your eyes and envision the situation as if it's happening on a stage and you're the director of this play. As you're watching the players, how might you make changes to the plot for an equitable outcome?

- Draw a diagram or Mind Map of the situation. As you work with it, your awareness will move into your cerebral brain and you'll begin to see alternatives and choices. Include these new choices in your diagram or Mind Map.

- Use a visual tool, such as a Tarot or oracle card. Select a card at random from the deck and describe what's happening in the picture. What choices do the people on the card have in regard to their situation? How does this relate to your situation?

Living in a choiceful state of being gives you the ability to have a creative array of options available to you at all times, allowing you to continue moving forward toward creating your best life.

Working with Fear

Fear isn't always something you want to ignore, get over, remove, or change into something more agreeable. Often, fear can be a most valuable ally.

Throughout this book there are exercises designed to assist you not only in identifying your fear, but working with it. Yes, that's correct. Working *with* your fear.

We were provided with fear as one of the most valuable tools in our Human Survival Toolkit. Although fear initially served the purpose of keeping us alive (the Reptilian brain's mode of survival), it has evolved and now serves some very important functions, as you'll soon discover.

The first step in working with fear is to identify it. Everyone experiences fear in many diverse ways. The following exercise helps you become aware of the many faces that fear appears specifically to you.

Putting a Face on Your Fears

Since most fears today are based on invisible foes, such as rejection or failure, it can be very tricky to spot how it shows up in your life. Fear has the talent of shape-shifting into an endless variety of forms, such as:

- Procrastination

- Perfectionism

- Laziness

- Self-doubt

- Making other things more important (such as sharpening all the pencils)

- Allowing others to sabotage your work

- Sabotaging your own work

- Easily being distracted from your work

- A sudden urge to watch TV or eat chocolate

- Anger

- Resentment

- Frustration

As you can see, fear doesn't always give you sweaty palms, make you all shivery, or weaken your knees. Fear is *anything* that stops you from moving forward, no matter how trivial that thing may seem.

It's vitally important for you to recognize how fear shows up in your life so that you can deal with it and stop *it* from stopping *you*. Unidentified, fear has free rein and can run rampant over your life.

So, how does fear show its face to you? Begin to find out now.

In the space below, list as many faces of fear as you can think of. No matter how small or insignificant it may be, add it to the list of faces that fear shows itself to you. If you're not comfortable writing in this book, use a separate sheet of paper or a notebook.

1.

2.

3.

4.

5.

6.

7.

8.

9.

10.

When you're done, use this list as a reference. Keep your list handy, adding to it as you discover more ways that fear shows up in your life. Remember to list everything from the mildest form to the biggest and scariest.

Faces of Other People's Fears

Now why, you might ask, would you give even one whit about other people's fears? The answer is simple: their fears can easily become your fears.

As you begin moving forward on your path of living your best life, everyone you know will be more than happy to share with you their fear about the choices you're making. Their intent may not be to burden you with their fear. They may innocently wish to protect you from having any similar bad experiences like the ones they had when they tried to do something challenging.

Nevertheless, there is a very real possibility that sharing their fear with you results in you consciously or unconsciously adopting their fears. Once you acquire fears from other people, they live within you, ever at the ready to tell you how stupid, selfish, inconsiderate, incompetent, or mean you are to even be *thinking* about doing whatever you have planned.

There's one quick and easy way to recognize these adopted fears: their voice is the second one you hear when you think about doing what you love or a choice you want to make. The first voice is your true Higher Self.

This fear-filled voice of another person has been called many things, such as the Gremlin, the Inner Critic, the English Teacher, Mr. Black Hat, and Yeahbut. Whatever you call it, know this:

that voice is not your voice
and that fear is not your fear.

Catching Fear

"My boss was so mean to me today, I just wanted to punch him in the nose."

"I was so mad when she said that, I just wanted to slap her silly."

"We got in an argument and I was so angry, if we hadn't been driving down the freeway, I would have jumped out of the car."

While these comments appear to be anger, the truth is they're all fear.

Anger is one of the most common faces of fear. It's also how most people deal with their fear.

Unfortunately, all too often anger isn't handled in a healthy way. Most typically, it gets stuffed. But it always finds a way out... usually in a manner more harmful and harsher than if it were dealt with directly.

When fear continues, it becomes frustration. If the fear is not alleviated, frustration grows larger and becomes anger, which can grow into full-blown rage. Riots are a perfect example of this process.

We're currently experiencing many disasters - natural and man-made - that are causing many people to become fearful. Unless the fear is dealt with, it can turn into frustration which can then grow into raging anger.

While there is typically little that one person can do to avert these disasters, there is much that can be done to relieve the fear caused by them.

First, know that fear is contagious. You can catch it from other people.

Watching news on TV is one way of catching fear. It isn't sex that sells ads in news programs on TV... it's fear. TV news is nothing but a list of disasters, all of which adds to the fear in those who watch.

Reading about the disasters in the newspapers is another way to catch fear. Big, blazing headlines on newspapers about the most recent violent events, the sorry state of our nation's economy and politics, and other scary stories, grab the attention of readers by activating fear within them.

Friends, coworkers, and others share their "fear germs" as they communicate their concerns about current events and how they might be affected. Pay attention to the words they use (always, never, everyone, etc.) and correct their language silently within your own thoughts or say to yourself "that's not true." This neutralizes the fear germs they're sharing with you.

Avoid people who are chronically fearful and negative. Anyone who lowers your energy and your emotions when you're around them is to be avoided as much as is practical. There are too many uplifting people in the world for you to remain in the company of those who create fear and other harmful emotions within you, simply by their presence.

Emotional Energy Fields

Recently when I was working out at the local gym, I found myself being very angry with one particular man who was on one of the machines near me. It wasn't that he was doing anything so wrong. I was just really angry with him for something so minor that I normally would have not even noticed.

Later, when I was home and away from the situation I reviewed my feelings in relation to the situation. Clearly, my anger was an over-reaction. What in the world could have caused me to feel such an intense emotion over such a nothing?

Of course! (slap to the forehead) The emotional energy field!

The man had been extremely hostile and angry and the closer I got to him, the more agitated I became. The reason was that I was feeling the anger in his emotional energy field.

We all have an emotional energy field, also called a morphogenic field. Most of the time we're unaware of these fields - ours and other peoples'. It's only when we have occurrences such as the one I had that our attention is brought to the powerful influence of this field.

The energy field that surrounds your body in its normal state has a neutral emotional charge to it. In this state it's also very close to your body. When you feel an intense emotion, whether it's fear, anger, love, excitement, or joy, the field expands outward and can radiate as far as 52'.

Imagine, then, all the people at a political rally, sports event, or music festival. As their emotions grow so does the size of their morphogenic field. The fields begin to overlap one another, causing the emotions to build in intensity. As they build, layer by layer, the energy fields blend and become one huge group energy field.

Think back to some of the sports events or political demonstrations that have unexpectedly erupted into violence. The emotions of all those involved were intensified by the highly charged group emotional field.

These examples are all fairly obvious to an observer. Anyone could see how excited the people in these groups were. However, there may be times when another person won't be exhibiting an emotion, yet their emotional energy field will affect you adversely.

Several years ago I was at the post office and saw a friend. I went over to her and we chatted for a while. She seemed happy and said that things were going very well for her. After we said our goodbyes I suddenly realized that I was feeling very sad. This was most odd because just minutes previous I had been feeling great. It was a warm, summer day and I had just received a large check - life was good. What, then, could possibly have caused this almost instant change of emotions?

Ah. My friend.

I was happy before I saw her but immediately after we parted company I was very sad. I discovered later that although she appeared happy, in reality she was very unhappy about her marriage. Although she was hiding her emotions, they were being radiated outward and were held in her morphogenic field. When we were chatting, I was being affected by the energy of the sadness she was radiating.

Want to protect yourself from being influenced by other people's emotional energy fields? The key is awareness. Being able to recognize when you're being unduly influenced by the emotions allows you to free yourself from inappropriate emotions that have no purpose for you.

Play with the following exercise to gain experience feeling someone else's energy field:

You'll need two people (obviously!). Stand about 15' or 20' apart, facing each other. Make sure you have a clear path between the two of you. One will be the Senser and one will be the Sender.

The person who is the Sender sets the boundary of their energy field somewhere between them and where the Senser is standing. This can be done by visualizing it or by simply setting your intent or imagining where it is. However it's done, the Senser must not know where the edge of the Sender's energy field is located. When the Sender has set their energy field they let the Senser know.

The Senser closes their eyes and begins to slowly walk toward the Sender, stopping when they feel or sense what they think is the edge of the Sender's energy field.

Switch roles with the Sender becoming the Senser and do it again. Play with it and have fun.

The more you do this, the easier it will be for you to recognize when you're being affected by someone else's emotional energy. As you become more adept at this you'll be able to more quickly set up protection from those energies you don't wish to affect you.

Talking with Fear

There are some very creative methods for silencing the voices of fear, one of which is the exercise that follows.

In one of the previous exercises (Putting a Face on Your Fear), you identified some of the faces of your fears, bringing them from the dark unknown into the bright light of reality. Using that information you can now work with your fear and use it to your advantage.

Fear serves a more subtle, yet no less important, duty in your life today beyond just keeping you alive. Fear alerts you to a wide variety of potential dangers beyond the physical, such as fear of humiliation, failure, not being loved, rejection, and abandonment.

However, fear will often put you on alert to protect you from something that no longer exists, never did exist, or is no longer valid in your life.

How will you know whether the fear you're experiencing is valid or not?

Simple. Just ask.

Using the Conversation with Fear exercise which follows on the next page, have a little talk with your fear. You may be surprised at the volume of information that wants to come forth.

Conversation with Fear

For this exercise write your questions and answers in longhand. This is very important. Here's why:

Printing is mostly composed of short, abrupt, disconnected lines while longhand is primarily connected circles and loops. When you print, you lift the pen from the paper, often several times during the creation of a single letter. This breaks the energy flow of the body/mind connection and puts a stop to your creative thinking.

Writing in longhand, or cursive, allows the information to flow more easily as your pen gently flows across the paper, only lifting from it or stopping when you reach the end of a word. When you're using longhand to write, the body/mind connection is much more clear than when you're printing, allowing for a smoother energy flow between your creative mind and your writing hand.

When you're ready to start, take a few moments to center yourself so you can focus better on this exercise. You may wish to take a few slow, deep breaths to aid you.

Then, when you feel ready, select one of the faces of fear that you identified in the previous exercise (Putting a Face on Your Fear). As you write your answers to the following questions, don't be overly concerned about the appearance of your handwriting. As long as you can read it enough to get the general gist of the information, the quality of your handwriting is sufficient. You can make corrections and notations for clarity after you're done writing.

Begin by asking your fear the first question below. When you're complete with the answer from the first question, continue on through each of the questions. Wait for a few moments between questions to insure that all the information has come forth.

Who are you?

What are you protecting me from?

How can you help me achieve my goals now?

What is the learning you give me?

When you feel that the answers you received from your fear are complete, re-read what you've written. This is a good time to fix any illegible words.

Use this exercise whenever a new face of fear shows up in your life. Focus on what the fear thinks it's protecting you from and how it can help you to move forward as you create a higher quality life for yourself.

The Bottom of Your Fear

There will be occasions when having a nice little chat with your fear won't be enough. Sometimes you'll need to face your fear and charge smack dab into it. It's during these times when you absolutely *must* dive down to the bottom of your fear before you can begin to work with it.

This exercise will assist you to continue past the shallow surface of your fear, going deeper and deeper until you've hit the bottom and can't go any further. Although this may seem challenging, you may be happily amazed at the results. The better you know your fear, the more easily you can lessen any power it may have over you. You can then use the fear as your ally to achieve your goals.

My own experience during a session with a mentor coach serves as an example of how effective this exercise is. During the session I was working on becoming unafraid to ask big, bold questions of my clients. My mentor coach opened the conversation by informing me that I was doing my clients a disservice by being so timid and fearful myself. She then asked me what would happen to me if I asked a bold question of my clients.

"They'd get mad at me." I answered.

"And then what would happen?" she retorted.

"They wouldn't like me."

"And then what?"

"They'd go away."

"And then what would happen?"

"I'd be lonely because no one would want to be around me because they don't like me asking them those kinds of questions."

"And then what would happen?"

"I'd be so lonely I wouldn't want to live anymore. I'd die from lack of love."

"And then what?"

"*I'm DEAD!* There is no *and then what*!"

"Yeah. Then what?"

"Well, I guess I'd go to Heaven and be in the presence of God."

"OK, let me get this straight," she said. "If you ask bold questions of your clients the worst thing that can happen to you is that you'll get to go to Heaven and hang out with God?"

Silence. Then laughter.

Yes, that got rid of my fear and I now ask bold questions of my clients - without hesitation.

Now it's your turn. The Fear Continuum Exercise on the next page is the same process my mentor coach used on me.

The Fear Continuum Exercise

You may want to have a friend or your life coach assist you with this exercise by asking the prodding questions and writing your answers for you. If someone is not available to help you, write your answers as you receive them. Remember to move quickly through this exercise in order to keep your Gremlin from interfering.

Begin by selecting an occasion during which you were stopped from moving forward because of fear. For this exercise, the bigger the fear the better.

Describe the action you wished to take and what stopped you.

Now, imagine what will happen to you if you continue on with this action despite your fear.

As you're working through this exercise, **it's very important that you keep going until you've absolutely hit bottom.** Continue until you can't go any further and you're at the very last thing that will happen to you. You may even have to go beyond dying, as I did during my mentored call.

What might happen to you if you don't let your fear stop you?

And after that, what will happen to you?

And then what?

What will happen to you after that?

And then what will happen to you?

Keep going until you absolutely can't go any further. Then, when you think you've truly found bottom, ask yourself one more time...

And then what?

Now summarize what you discovered by completing this sentence:

The very worst thing that will happen to me if I...

is...

Repeat this exercise anytime you find yourself going around and around the same old circle with the same old fear. Discovering the worst thing that can happen to you if you ignore your fear is the best thing you can do.

Fears grow in the dark. Bring your fears to the light so you can examine them closely and diminish their power.

Balancing Fear

You have within you a self-regulating scale that keeps a perfect balance between the amounts of desirable and undesirable emotions that you allow yourself to feel.

If you could weigh the emotions you feel, then you might allow yourself to feel, say, ten pounds of fear. This also means that your self-balancing scale will allow you to feel ten pounds of whatever you think is the opposite of fear - love, joy, happiness, courage, etc. Ten pounds exactly of fear. Ten pounds exactly of its opposite. No more. No less.

People who are "more emotional" don't have more emotions. They're just more willing to feel greater amounts of emotion at both ends of the scale.

Although people who allow themselves to feel only small amounts of emotion are said to be emotionally balanced, it is a misconception. **Everyone is emotionally balanced.** Some just have larger balancing scales than others.

Artists and other creatives, who are often stereotyped in our society as being emotionally out of balance, are just as balanced emotionally as those who allow themselves a very miniscule amount of emotional feeling. They simply allow themselves to experience more tonnage of emotions on both sides of the neutral balance point. They feel more pain *and* more joy, more anger *and* more compassion, more love *and* more hurt... all in perfect balance to each other.

Living your life to the fullest means that you'll be experiencing new levels of emotion, both highs *and* lows. As you expand your life you'll find yourself becoming more impassioned, which means that you'll be feeling more joy, happiness, and excitement.

It also means that you'll be experiencing more on the opposite end of the scale, such as more doubt, anger, and fear.

The Emotional Scale exercise illustrates this principle more clearly.

The Emotional Scale

100
FEAR
0
100

This image represents an emotional scale. Notice that each side of the scale has a value of from 0 to 100.

FEAR is on the left side of the scale. What's at the opposite end of your scale from fear? Joy? Happiness? Courage? Write the name of it under the 100 on the far end of the scale on the right side.

Now, recall a time when you were faced with doing something new and felt fear about your ability to actually do this new thing. Rate the intensity of that fear from 1 to 100.

Next, on the FEAR side of the scale, between the zero at the central balance point on the line below and the maximum of 100, insert a marker that represents approximately the amount or intensity of fear that you experienced during that incident.

Now, insert a marker on the opposite side of the scale, rating the opposite emotion of your fear at exactly the same distance from the 0 point, or neutral, as you rated your fear.

How would you like to move that indicator outward on your scale and feel more of whatever the opposite of fear is for you? Remember, this means that you'll also be moving the indicator for fear outward as well.

If you're up to the challenge, then read on.

Comfort Zones and Sabotage

Whenever you're taken beyond your emotional comfort zone (the space between your markers for fear and its opposite on your emotional scale) you'll do whatever it takes, use whatever remedies you have available, to bring yourself back into the measure of emotion that's comfortable to you.

This action of returning to the emotional comfort zone is called "self medication" and it can take many forms: alcohol, drugs, coffee, sugar, work, sex, TV, etc.

The most common belief held about self-medication is that it's used to avoid or reduce undesirable feelings, such as pain, fear, and anger. However, **self medication is also used to avoid feeling too good.**

When you're taken out of your comfort zone on the feel-good side of the emotional scale, your subconscious mind knows this means that at some point you'll also be taken out of your comfort zone on the feel-bad side. This is the self-balancing scale at work. You don't want to feel bad emotions more intensely than you've become accustomed to, so you self-medicate and self regulate yourself back into the safety of your emotional comfort zone.

If you've ever found yourself saying, "This is too good to be true" or "I can't believe this," it means that you've just been taken out of your comfort zone on the feel-good side of the scale. As soon as you hear these phrases, or something similar, know that your automatic balancing system is preparing to swing you back into the comfort zone of your emotional scale.

Soon, you'll probably hear words coming from your mouth such as, "I knew it was too good to last". The next thing you know, you're sitting on the inside of your comfort zone on your perfectly balanced emotional scale.

This is the point at which you'll see your weight loss plans fail, your exercise programs fall apart, and your new-found strengths scaring you into retreating back to your emotional comfort zone. Sabotage, whether from your conscious mind, your subconscious mind, or someone else's mind, is a form of self medication. It allows you to move back into your old familiar emotional comfort zone.

Your subconscious mind doesn't want you to feel *too* good because if you do, it knows that a bad feeling is lurking just around the corner.

Living your life free of fear isn't about you being trapped in the self-imposed prison of your comfort zone, watching TV until your brains fall out. It means you'll be expanding into a broader scale of emotions, both good and bad, to *fully* experience your life. When you're living your life to the fullest, you'll experience the entire range and volume of emotions.

How much more joy, excitement, happiness, _____ (fill in the blank with your choice of feel-good emotion) would you like to experience?

100
FEAR

0

100

Refer to The Emotion Scale in which you previously inserted your markers as a baseline. Using the Emotion Scale above, insert new markers indicating where you would *really* like to be on The Emotional Scale. You may want to use different colored pens for where you are now and where you would like to be.

Then answer these questions:

What would you need to change in order to be at the new level?

What steps might you take to experience the richness of all your emotions?

What will you be doing differently when you're at the new level?

When you experience your new levels of emotion, good and bad, remember that you'll be out of your comfort zone.

If things get to be too much for you and you find yourself wanting to jump back into the safety of your comfort zone, return to the Conversation with Fear and the Fear Continuum exercises. Use these two exercises to explore your new and higher level of fear so that you gain the new wisdom that it's offering you.

Turning Weakness into Strength

Everyone has something they don't like about themselves and you're no exception. No doubt you have qualities and attributes about yourself that you wish you didn't have or could change.

Although you may think of these qualities as fearful weaknesses, *all* qualities have both an undesirable *and* a desirable side to them. For instance, a desirable quality like leadership can also be viewed in an undesirable light as being too controlling. Flexibility can be seen as being wishy-washy. Tidiness or orderliness can be seen as nit-picky.

All undesirable qualities are actually desirable qualities with the volume turned up too high. When you turn the volume down on an undesirable quality, it becomes a desirable quality. Turn down the volume on wishy-washy and you have flexibility. Reduce the volume on nit-picky and you have tidy. Softening control makes it a leadership quality.

What are some of the qualities about yourself that you view as being your weaknesses or undesirable traits? In the space on the next page or in your notebook, list at least five of them.

48

1.

2.

3.

4.

5.

Now, under each trait you identify as a weakness, list at least three qualities that turn it into a strength for you... once you've turned the volume down a bit.

Keep this list handy for use when you come to a standstill and fearfully think (mistakenly, of course) that you just don't have what it takes to deal with whatever challenge you're facing. Then use it to remind yourself of all the wonderful strengths that you truly do possess.

You might want to make copies of it and post them in places where you'll see your strengths often, such as on the wall of your office, on your refrigerator door, and on your bathroom mirror.

F.E.A.R.

False **E**vidence **A**ppearing **R**eal

The situation is never the issue. No matter how it appears on the surface, there is a greater truth lying underneath.

When your boss gets mad at you for something you did or didn't do, the anger isn't about you, your action, or non-action. The anger you see is False Evidence Appearing Real. In this example, it's likely that the fear your boss is experiencing is that he could be held accountable for the situation that results in suffering a reprimand. Or worse.

Because all fear is sited in the future, your boss is envisioning the worst-case scenario of his future and then projecting the resultant fear (anger) onto you. The false evidence in this case is that your boss is angry. In reality, what your boss really is experiencing is fear. Remove the possibility of future repercussions for your boss, which is the real basis of the fear, and the anger/fear dissipates.

Reflect back to a situation in which you were experiencing one of the faces of fear.

Describe the situation on the next page or in your notebook.

Then answer the following questions:

What was the face of fear that showed up?

What was the False Evidence Appearing Real (F.E.A.R.)?

What new insights did you gain by viewing the incident from this fresh perspective?

The Fear of Not Having Enough

The fear of not having enough is directly related to the fear of not being worthy or deserving. This is the same fear that manifests as poverty consciousness and keeps people in bare-bones survival mode.

That inner voice you hear chattering away inside of you, saying that you can't have the very things you desire most is keeping you from having not only those particular desires, but also *all* the wondrous things that you deserve.

This voice may be the result of beliefs you've been programmed with that have originated from your parents, family, teachers, religious leaders, and friends. If so, you're living your life according to the beliefs of other people. This means you're living someone else's life.

This inner voice varies in volume, tone, and persistence in each person and in each event. It may be a tiny, distant voice that occasionally whines, or a looming, booming, constantly nagging voice. Usually it's somewhere in between. Whatever it sounds like, though, it's consistent in telling you what you *"should"* think, feel, and do.

The important point here is that it's not *your* voice.

You couldn't possibly be that mean to yourself, could you?

Of course not.

That's why you're here now, working at releasing all the irrelevant causes of fear in your life that aren't yours. Fears that are nevertheless causing your forward movement toward creating your best life to be blocked or stymied.

The next exercise, The Take-Away Game, will assist you in gaining clarity about those hidden voices that are keeping you from getting all the good that you deserve.

The Take-Away Game

This exercise helps you to clearly identify what your Gremlin, Inner Critic, Mr. Blackhat, or Yeahbut is saying in an effort to keep you from having what you desire.

Select something big, something that you think is out of reach for you but nonetheless is something that you *really* desire. It can be something physical, such as a new boat or car, or something intangible, such as self-confidence or peace of mind.

Now, *very quickly*, before your Inner Critic has a chance to rudely interrupt you, complete the following *without hesitation*:

I can't have it because

I can't have it because

I can't have it because

I can't have it because

I can't have it because

I don't deserve it because

I don't deserve it because

I don't deserve it because

I don't deserve it because

I don't deserve it because

Review what you've written and notice how each of these statements reflects a face of fear. For greater understanding of how fear is stopping you, on the next page write your answers to the questions.

What are the particular faces of fear that showed up? List as many as you can.

Which of these fears that are about what you can't have and don't deserve sound like other people's voices? (This is a trick question. *All* of these fears are from other people. Your true, Divine self knows without a molecule of doubt that you deserve to have whatever you desire.)

Whose voices are they? Note the name(s) of the person or people who are the source of the negative voice next to the fear they shared with you.

When you get all these thoughts and beliefs about why you can't have what you want out of your head and in front of you in black and white, you can see them for what they are - False Evidence Appearing Real. FEAR!

Rescinding Vows That No Longer Serve You

The thoughts and beliefs that keep you from moving forward to gain what you desire may be programming from a past lifetime when you took a vow of poverty that's still in effect. Even though those vows are no longer relevant or necessary, you've somehow never rescinded or cancelled them and they're still functioning.

An important first step in shifting those fearful beliefs and thoughts is to rid yourself of vows that are blocking your forward progress. These vows may be those you once made that are no longer beneficial, valuable, or even valid to you as you create your best life.

Releasing past vows that are no longer relevant is a necessary step to clearing old beliefs that block you from allowing yourself to have what you want.

The way your vows were created, the time when they were created, and their purposes are infinitely unique.

- The past vow may be from this lifetime or a past lifetime.

- It might be an official, ceremonial, or ritualistic vow, such as a vow of poverty taken as part of the requirements for you to become a member of a religious sect.

- The vow may have been stated very casually, such as when you may have said simply and innocently, "Well! I'm never going to do that again." That being taking a chance on a financial opportunity, trying something new and daring, beginning a relationship with someone out of your ordinary style, or something else new and different.

Whatever the vow and however you created it, you'll find life becomes more joyful and satisfying when you don't have fear-filled vows attached to you, holding you back from getting and having what you desire.

Ridding yourself of restrictive vows is quick and easy. You simply craft a rescission of the vow you wish to rescind and state it aloud. You may want to do something extra, such as light a white candle, burn incense, add "so be it" to the end, or anything else that will enhance the meaning of this process for you.

Following are some sample rescissions that you can use as is, add to them, or change the wording in order to make them more personal and powerful for you.

"I hereby rescind any and all vows that I've taken in the past, whether known or unknown to me, that are inappropriate for me now and are blocking my forward movement toward fully living my highest and best life."

"I command rescission of all vows I have ever made, in ignorance or in truth, that are no longer assisting my higher good. I ask that all restrictions be lifted and eliminated so that I can align with my highest purpose."

"I now declare all vows and contracts null and void in this incarnation and all incarnations across space and time. Spirit, release all structures, devices, entities, orientations or effects associated with these vows and contracts NOW!"

If you wish, you may write your own rescissions in the space below or your notebook. Refer to your recissions often and repeat as is needed.

Taking the Fear Out
of Making Decisions

It doesn't matter if a decision is small or large, **all decisions are stressful**. And stress is just one of the many faces of fear.

In my work as a Life Purpose Coach I've discovered tools and techniques to help my clients relieve the stress involved in the need for choices and decisions that are necessary for them to make.

Here's three of my favorites:

#1. Urgent/Important Some decisions are important, some are urgent, and some are both. The difference is the amount of time you have before the decision must be made.

So, the first step is to define the time limits for urgent and important. At what point does a decision become important – or urgent? Does urgent mean it has to be done within a day or an hour? Note that each decision will probably have an different time limit, so you may wish to perform this exercise for each one.

When you've defined both urgent and important to your satisfaction, get four sheets of paper and insert one of the following titles at the top of each sheet of paper:

Urgent *and* Important

Urgent *but not* Important

Important *but not* Urgent

Not Urgent *or* Important

Now, list all the choices and decisions you need to make regarding an issue and insert them on the appropriate paper.

You'll be greatly relieved when you're finished to discover everything doesn't all have to be done today! (TIP: If *everything* is under "Urgent and Important", you need to redefine those two terms.)

#2. The TimeLine Create a list of all the choices or decisions you need to make regarding a project or an issue. Next to each decision insert the date by when the decision needs to be made. When you're complete with the list, reorder it into a sequential timeline beginning at the current date and continuing to completion.

#3. The Truthful Body If the act of making a decision throws you into the heebie jeebies, here's a simple yet amazingly accurate technique for making a decision:

Envision one of your choices. If it's a thing, such as a color you want to paint the house or a new car you want, envision it as if it's already done. If the choice is about you doing something, envision yourself actually doing it.

Now, quickly scan your body for physical sensations and/or emotions and feelings. Do you feel a sense of dread or anxiety? Joy or excitement? Discomfort in your stomach? Tension in your shoulders or neck?

Does your energy rise or fall? Make note of any and all sensations – physical and emotional – this visual creates within your body.

Next, envision another choice. When you clearly have the vision, again quickly scan your body for physical sensations and/or feelings.

The choice that makes you feel good is the correct and appropriate one for you. Your body knows the truth and, unlike your conscious mind, will never lie to you.

Try these techniques the next time you need to make a decision and are all stressed out about it. You'll be sooooo relieved! And less fearful each time you're confronted with a decision that you need to make, too.

Empowering Language

Words have power beyond their importance as a communication method. Each word you speak has a vibrational signature that triggers certain responses, memories, and thought processes in the people who are receiving the energy of your words.

These people receiving the energy of your words include you.

The words you use to describe your version of reality are heard not only by others, but more importantly by you. As you speak, your ears are hearing what you say. As you write your words, your eyes are reading them. You, too, are receiving the vibrations and the message of your own words.

Words are not just bits of communication. They're tools with which you're programming your life.

The language you habitually use affects not only how you communicate with yourself and others, it affects how you experience your life. You create your reality with the words you choose.

Change Your Language and Change Your Life

The language you use can empower you and put you in control of your life.

It can also have the opposite effect.

It can disempower you, placing you in victim position and at the mercy of other people and their wants, desires, and whims. Further, disempowering language makes you a victim of circumstances, events, and your environment. In other words, your words can create a fear-based reality for yourself.

By consciously changing the disempowering words you've been habitually using into empowering words, you can change your life. Yes, it's that simple.

In the chart below are both disempowering and empowering words and phrases. Use the empowering words on the right to replace the disempowering words you have been using.

Disempowering	Empowering
should	choose, desire, want, could
need to, have to	want to, choose to, desire to
can't	am not willing to, choose not to
always, never	sometimes, often, seldom
must	choose, desire
but	and
try	intend, aim
you make me	I feel, I am
if only	next time
problem	opportunity, challenge

Take the Empowering Language Challenge!

This exercise gives you experience in replacing disempowering words with those that empower you. The more you practice this, the easier empowering language will come to you.

1. Use a disempowering word or phrase, such as "should" or "have to" in a sentence. An example might be, "I should mow the lawn" or "I have to mow the lawn."

2. Say the disempowering statement out loud, and take a moment to notice how you feel. Pay attention to whether you feel lighter or heavier, more energetic or less, filled with joy and happiness or with dread and anxiety. Notice the tone and volume of your voice.

3. Now, reword the statement using a word from the empowering language column and say the statement out loud. Notice how your voice sounds this time as opposed to how it sounded the first time.

How do you feel when you use the empowering language as opposed to when you used the disempowering language?

"Shoulding" All Over Yourself

"Should" is probably the most used of all the self-abusive disempowering words. It's so common that most people don't even realize they're using it.

Here are a few examples:

"Well, I should get off the phone now and get back to work."

"She should know better."

"I should call them and thank them."

"Somebody should do something about this." (*This* is the ultimate victim statement, insinuating that the speaker has no power to do anything about the situation.)

Here's the truth about "should." The voice you hear telling you what you "should" and "shouldn't" do is not your voice. It's somebody else's voice telling you what *they* want you to do.

This person may or may not actually be in front of you. Typically, the voice with the "should" is one that's still hanging around from your childhood. When you were growing up, you were told you "should" do something or "shouldn't" do something else in order to be a good little child. Your inner child is still trying to be that good little girl or boy by doing what it thinks it "should" be doing. As an adult, you still think that doing what you "should" will make you a good person.

It doesn't. It makes you resentful, frustrated, angry, and depressed and fearful.

Ironically, rather than motivating you, "shoulding" sets up resistance within you, almost guaranteeing that whatever you "should" do, you won't. "Should" has nothing to do with reality. As soon as you hear a "should," you can expect that whatever follows will most likely not occur.

The following exercise will give you greater insight into how and when you use "should" and the results... or lack thereof.

1. In your notebook, list some of the "shoulds" or "shouldn'ts" that you commonly use on yourself. Next to each "should" note whose voice it is. Who told you these "shoulds"?

2. What would you like to change these "shoulds" into? (Refer to the Disempowering/Empowering list.) Write it below the related "should" in your notebook. As you're working with these "shoulds", how are they affecting your energy level? Notice any differences in how your body feels as you change them, especially around your stomach and neck.

3. How have these "shoulding" messages affected your choices in the past? What results have they produced or not produced?

4. What are some of the "shoulds" or "shouldn'ts" that are currently being used on you by other people?

Power Down Negative Emotions

You are *not* a helpless, fear-driven victim of your emotions. You have the power to increase or decrease the energy charge that accompanies emotions such as anger, fear, and depression.

Just like the use of empowering language, all it takes to control the intensity of your emotions is changing the words you habitually use to describe what you're feeling. You can choose to diffuse the intensity of your emotions by describing them with words that are less volatile.

The ability to defuse your emotions at will is very useful and powerful. There are times when it's simply not appropriate or beneficial to blow your stack or burst into tears. You may be in an important meeting or dealing with a valued customer when you suddenly feel your anger flare over something that was said by another. Reducing the intensity of your emotion allows you to function more efficiently than if you gave all control away to your anger.

By decreasing the intensity of your emotions with your choice of language, whether spoken aloud to others or silently to yourself, you can remain calmer and more emotionally stable. When you're emotionally stable you can continue to think creatively and logically.

When circumstances are more suitable, such as in the privacy of your home, you can luxuriate in a full-blown rant. But if you habitually allow yourself to intensify your negative emotions with the careless use of your language, you're wasting precious energy on something that is not productive. Additionally, you are creating fear within yourself.

The point is that you have the power to choose how much of any emotion you wish to feel. You are not a powerless victim of your emotions. You can increase or decrease the intensity of them according to how you choose to describe them, both to yourself and to others.

Below is a chart of some negative emotional expressions as they're commonly used. Next to them are some alternatives that you can use to reduce the intensity of them.

Note: This exercise is not designed to turn a negative into a positive. Nor is it intended to stop your emotions. Its purpose is to allow you to feel the emotion, while controlling the level of intensity so you can still function.

When you find that your emotions are inhibiting you from functioning at your best, take a deep breath and power down the emotion by choosing the words you use to describe how you're feeling – both to yourself and to others.

You'll find that you instantly feel less of the negative emotions. After all, who can feel furiously angry when using the word "peeved" to describe how they feel?

Negative Expression	Less Intense
I'm angry	I'm disenchanted, peeved
I'm afraid	I'm uncomfortable
I'm depressed	I'm on the road to a turn-around
I'm destroyed	I'm set back
I'm disgusted	I'm surprised
I'm furious	I'm annoyed, I'm fascinated
I'm hurt	I'm bothered
I'm exhausted	I'm not very energetic right now
I'm nervous	I'm energized, I'm stimulated
I'm overwhelmed	I have many opportunities I'm in demand
I'm petrified	I'm challenged
I'm sick	I'm cleansing
I'm stupid	I'm learning
I'm scared	I'm excited
I'm stressed	I'm fully engaged, I'm alive
I'm scared to death	I'm moving and shaking
I'm frustrated	I'm regrouping

Try a few of these to see how effective they are. State out loud one of the powered up negative statements on the left. Then take a moment as you sense how you feel.

Now state aloud the powered down version. How do you feel now? Do you sense the lowered intensity of emotional energy in your body?

Shifting your language so it's less powerful in the negative sense not only keeps you from feeling negative, fearful emotions, it also affects the energy and emotions of those around you. Imagine the response you'll get when you state to those around you that you're annoyed rather than announcing that you're furious or livid with anger.

Notice how you typically describe your negative emotions. If they're not on the list above, add them and then create an alternative that's less intense. Practice saying the alternatives until you're comfortable with them.

If you find there are some words that you just can't get comfortable saying, create your own alternative language to power down the intensely negative statement.

Turbo-charge Your Language

As you're now learning, words have the power to change your energy. You know that empowering language will take you out of victim stance - an energy sucking, fear-filled position if there ever was one. You also know how to diminish your negative emotions by shifting the words you use to describe how you feel to less intense versions.

Now you'll learn how to use words to *increase* your positive energy and that of others around you, simply by choosing the words to describe how you're feeling.

For example, what is your typical response when someone asks you, "How are you?" What words do you habitually use to answer them?

Do you usually say, "oh, fine," in a tone of voice that drops to the ground or is much less than enthusiastic? If so, each time you answer like that you're bringing your own energy - and the energy of others around you - down to the ground along with your tone of voice.

How about raising everyone's energy instead?

On the chart below are some words and phrases that are common responses people use when they meet and ask "How are you?" To the right are some alternatives to raise your energy and that of others around you.

Good	GREAT!
I'm all right	I'm superb
I'm fine	I'm awesome
I'm good	I'm great
I'm great	I'm incredible
I'm excited	I'm ecstatic
I'm cool	I'm outrageous
I'm happy	I'm in Heaven!
I'm hangin' in there	I'm fabulous!

Experience the difference now. State aloud your normal response to the "How are you?" question. Take a moment to sense how your energy feels.

Now choose a turbo-charged response and state it out loud. Did you notice a difference in your level of energy after you used the turbo-charged response?

Pick a couple of your favorite turbo-charged responses to "how are you?" Practice saying them until you're comfortable doing it.

For the next week, whenever someone asks you how you are, use the alternate and notice how you feel after you say your new response.

Notice also the difference in how people react to your new turbo-charged response.

Switching Your Focus

If you're feeling sad, irked, stymied, annoyed, depressed, frustrated, worried, fearful, _____ (fill in the blank with your favorite negative emotion) there's a technique you can use to feel better and it only takes about a nanosecond.

Lynn Grabhorn, author of *Excuse Me, Your Life Is Waiting*, called it "Flip-switching."

Abraham in *Ask and It Is Given* calls it the game of "Which Thought Feels Better?"

I call it "Switching Your Focus".

Whatever you want to call it, the process is simple, fast, and amazingly effective. Here's how it works:

1. When you notice that you're not feeling as happy as you'd like to be, consciously choose to think about something that gives you a better feeling.

That's it. Just one easy step. But don't be deceived by its simplicity. It's a multidimensional tool that does much more than just make you feel better for a short time.

Here's an example of how it works:

You're worried and stressed about your current financial situation and can't seem to stop yourself from fretting about money issues. Your thoughts loop over and over about how you don't have the money you want or need. Even though you've been doing the work - both physically and energetically - to create a greater income, you can't help wondering where it is. When will your manifesting show results with more money showing up in your life?

Now, switch your focus.

Think about those things that *are* going well for you now - things that make you feel happier. Focus on the parts of your work that you love, the relief or gratitude you feel when you receive payment for doing your work, the pride you feel when you pay your bills on time.

If that's too much of a stretch, look around at your environment right now. What do you see that you love... or even like? A photo of a loved one? The view from your window? The clothes you're wearing? Your screensaver on your computer monitor? The color of your nail polish?

As you shift your focus to something you like, you're making yourself feel better emotionally. As you feel better emotionally, you're raising your vibration.

As the Law of Attraction states, "that which is like unto itself is drawn." So, not only will you feel better, as a bonus your higher vibrational thoughts will attract things, situations, and people that contribute even more to your better feelings.

The result is that you'll feel happier more often and longer. And as you do so, you'll find a better quality of things, situations, and people coming into your life.

The quality of your life spirals upward each time you consciously choose to think a thought that gives you a better feeling.

The next time you catch yourself feeling an emotion you don't like, remember that **you're just one thought away from feeling better**... and improving your life as you do so.

If You Could...

What would you do if you knew you couldn't fail?

That's a popular buzz question that perpetually makes the rounds of motivational workshops, life coaching, and the like. I call it the Failure Question. The intent behind it is to help people discover what's holding them back from doing and having what they really, truly, deep down, want.

In many if not most cases, that question isn't appropriate to the circumstances simply because failing isn't always the issue. At least not in the beginning of any attempt for change.

Nor is it the only issue.

In fact, it's a very small percentage of the many reasons why people stay stuck in less than desirable circumstances and situations.

Usually the reasons most people have for not even beginning to attempt something new and challenging has nothing to do with failing. Other obstacles get in their way before they even begin to consider that they might fail.

The fear of failing often occurs to people only *after* they've stepped into action, if it occurs to them at all. Failing can be such a vast concept for many that they don't even recognize it as something that might happen to them. It's sort of like the "can't see the forest for the trees" adage.

Most of the unseen barriers that keep people from moving toward their dreams are much more specific and much more relative to their own circumstances and situations than over-all, blanket, one-type-fits-all failure.

When the Failure Question is reworded using more specific and appropriate reasons for staying frozen in the fearful state of stuckness, suddenly long buried dreams are unveiled... brought forth into the light of possibility.

Now and only now can the dreams be nurtured so they might grow into reality.

Here are some examples of new, more specific versions of the Failure Question:

- What would you love to do or have if you could afford it?

- If it was okay with your husband / wife / mate / boss / mother / father, what would you love to do?

- If you weren't too old (or too young) what would you like to do?

- What would you love to do if you had the time?

- If you had the education or degree, what you love to do?

What are some of your additional examples of this question?

Better yet, what are your answers?

Fear of Change

Life is all about change. What I've observed about change is that there are two types:

1. yours

2. theirs

When it's your idea to make a change, you're much more willing and enthusiastic about it than if it's somebody else's idea. Why? Because when it's your choice to initiate a change *you* are in control, but *they* are in control when it's their choice.

When change is someone else's idea, you may think that you have no choice in the matter. This is the pivotal moment when you give up your power of choice and step into the position of the fearfully powerless victim.

Know this: you always have choice in all matters. No one else can make you a victim. You become a victim by your own choice.

Being in victim stance is a state of fear. Although you can stifle the energy it won't make the fear go away. Instead, it escapes out a side door and usually takes some form of resentment. Passive aggressive behavior, snide and snippy comments, and sabotage are just a few of the side doors that victim energy takes.

What's the solution? Recognize that you have the power of choice in all matters, including change. When you're in a place of choice, you take back your power and move out of victim stance.

When change is instigated by other people, there are two areas in which you have the power of choice - you can change the thing *or* you can change your attitude/belief about it. Here's an example:

Someone has begun to build a house on the lot next to your home. You resent it because you'll be losing your privacy.

What you can do about the situation:

    1. Plant a privacy screen

    2. Build a fence

    3. Sell your house and move to one that's in the middle of 50 acres

What you can do about yourself:

    1. Do some inner exploration about what's so important to you about privacy

    2. Get clear on any other issues that may be involved at a deeper level about your need for privacy

    3. Be grateful about this opportunity to learn more about yourself and what's truly important to you

Likewise, you can overcome your fear of change by examining the choices you have around the situation and your beliefs about the matter.

You even have choices around how you can examine your choices! You might have a brainstorming session, create a mind map, meditate, or a combination of these.

Have fun and be curious as you explore your options and all the choices you DO have.

Personal Boundaries

Just exactly what are personal boundaries? The following is the most descriptive and accurate definition of personal boundaries I've found:

"Personal boundaries are invisible lines of protection you set around yourself to define what others are or are not allowed to do to you or in your presence."

Why are personal boundaries so important? Without them you lose your power of choice. This instantly places you in fear-filled victim stance

External influences such as other people's wants and desires, events and situations, your environment, time, and other influences lose their fearful impact and their power over you when you strengthen and uphold your personal boundaries.

These invisible lines protect you in all areas of life including:

Physical: This is anything regarding your physical body and physical belongings. It may range from not allowing others to use your possessions without your permission to not allowing strangers to harm your body.

Mental: This relates to all mental activity, including allowing others to determine what you think or believe about anything - specifically or generally.

Emotional: Anything that relates to your emotional well being is included in this area. An example is not allowing others to chronically dump on you with their emotional problems.

Spiritual: This includes boundaries that control the timing and methods of input you receive from your spiritual guides, the type of energy you will or will not allow around you, and much more.

How strong are your personal boundaries?

One easy way to discern if your personal boundaries need to be stronger is to take the following quiz. Write your answers in your notebook or workbook so you can total your score when you're finished.

1. Do other people in your life, such as your spouse, co-workers, friends, and family, always seem to be telling you how to live your life?

2. Do people often tell you how easy you are to get along with?

3. Do you suffer from stress related diseases such as high blood pressure, ulcers, fibromyalgia, or eating disorders?

4. Are you often made to feel smaller or less important by other people?

5. Does *everybody* like you?

6. Do you often find yourself telling other people what they need to do to fix a situation in their life?

7. Do people sometimes seem to be put off by questions that you ask them?

8. Do you often feel that other people take advantage of your kind and generous nature?

9. Are you the one at work who always gets the least desirable assignments?

10. Do you often feel angry after an encounter with another person and aren't exactly sure why?

Give yourself 1 point for every "yes" answer. Add up your YES answers for your score.

1-3 points: Fairly strong boundaries and could use some further strengthening.

4-6 points: Your boundaries are a little flabby and need work to get them muscled up.

7-10 points: Your boundaries are 90 pound weaklings! Start NOW to strengthen them!!

Awareness: The First Step for Strong Personal Boundaries

Right now you probably aren't aware of your boundaries until they've been grossly violated, totally ignored, or vastly infringed upon. Often it may not be until sometime after the fact that you realize you experiences a boundary invasion.

Red alerts, such as certain physical and emotional sensations, serve as warnings that one of your boundaries is being invaded. There's a variety of ways in which these boundary alerts can be experienced. Some of the most common red alerts are:

- **A physical discomfort somewhere in your body**, such as a sensation of being punched in the stomach or having the wind knocked out of your. Another common boundary alert is tenseness anywhere in your body, such as in your neck or jaw muscles. Common sayings such as, "I felt like I'd been kicked in the gut", or "It knocked the wind out of me," or "That just torques my jaws." are all responses to boundary invasions.

- **A sudden or growing anger** during an interaction with another person. The awareness of this alert can happen some time after the interchange, as often happens to people who are not yet cognizant of their personal boundaries.

- **A feeling of being made smaller or diminished in importance by another person**. This can be accompanied by a change in physiology, such as hunching the shoulders, curling up in a slouch, or collapsing the torso in an instinctive effort to protect the most vulnerable body parts from being harmed.

- **Being shocked or stunned by the actions of another**.

- **Wanting to escape** another person in some manner. This can take physical form, such as stepping backward or actually removing yourself from their presence. It can also be mental, such as suddenly finding yourself thinking about something else more pleasant.

Gaining awareness of how you sense boundary invasion and identifying your personal boundary alerts are the first and most important steps to building a healthy set of personal boundaries. The best way to gain this awareness is to revisit how you felt when you were having experiences that you suspect were boundary violations.

Think back to an experience you've had that was a less than satisfying communication with someone and which you now suspect was a violation of your personal boundaries. Then answer these questions:

1. What did you sense or feel as it was happening?

2. What did you feel or sense after it happened?

3. How did you react?

90

These sensations, no matter how insignificant you may deem them to be, are your boundary alerts. Write **all** of them in your notebook or workbook.

Repeat this exercise several more times using different experiences. Notice any trends or repeats. Then, for one week, practice noticing these symptoms of boundary invasion. Do nothing beyond simply noticing when you sense your boundary alerts and how you feel.

Continue this practice until you're familiar with the sensations of your personal boundary alerts and you feel fairly comfortable that you can quickly recognize when your boundaries are being infringed upon.

When you feel fairly comfortable that you can easily recognize your boundary alerts, you're ready for the next step: upholding your boundaries.

Upholding Your Personal Boundaries

There are three basic steps to upholding your boundaries:

1. Inform the violator of your personal boundary and, if appropriate, the life value that it honors. State it in a calm voice. Don't be angry, defensive, or sc-sc-sc-scared.

2. Ask them to honor your boundary. When you ask someone to *honor* your request, you're asking them to do more than just stop their annoying or disrespectful behavior. You're offering them the opportunity to *become* honorable. What a graceful way to request respect for your personal boundary. Who could resist?

3. Thank them. When you thank someone, typically it's for something they've already done. Thanking your personal boundary invader in advance of them honoring your boundary tells them this is a done deal. The assumption is that they *will* honor your boundary.

Sounds quite simple, doesn't it? However, at first it might be intimidating to state your boundary to someone, especially if they've been getting away with pushing you around for a considerable amount of time.

You may get a variety of reactions from people when you first begin to uphold your life values with your personal boundaries. Surprise, shock, and anger are a few of the responses that you may experience from your boundary invaders. After all, most of these people have been getting away with their disrespectful, dishonoring behavior of you for a long time. They may not be exactly elated about losing control over you.

When you get a reaction that's less than desirable to you when you uphold your personal boundary remember this:

Don't justify, rationalize, or apologize for your boundary.

Don't open it up to debate.

Don't fill in any stunned silences with an explanation as to why you're doing this.

Justifications, explanations, and apologies defuse the power of your boundaries, and render them worthless.

A simply worded statement of what your boundary is, how you want the violator to honor it, and a gracious "thank you" is all that's necessary or required to defend your boundary.

Below are four examples of ways to state your personal boundaries. Notice that they follow the three-step formula of informing the boundary invader, asking for compliance, and thanking them.

1. "_____is very important to me and I do not allow anyone to _____ in my presence. I ask you to honor this. Thank you.

2. _____ is one of the values that I live my life by. To honor this I do not allow anyone to _____ in my presence. Thank you."

3. "_____ is one of my most important values in life. I require that you honor my value by _____. Thank you."

4. "One of my most important life values is _____. It's how I choose to live my life. I ask you to honor my value by _____. Thank you."

Feel free to play with these examples, rearranging and changing the language so that you're comfortable using it. Practice saying these personal boundary requests daily, both in private and to someone you trust and are comfortable with.

When you're comfortable with the language, the act of informing others of your personal boundaries becomes so much easier for you. Then at the time to state your boundary, you won't be searching for the words or, worse yet, unable to speak at all because you don't know what to say.

Also, when you know how to say it in a way that will be heard and received by the boundary invader, you exude confidence, which increases your chances of getting agreement and compliance.

When you've practiced verbalizing your personal boundaries enough that you feel comfortable saying them, you're ready to try them out in real life.

One of the best methods for identifying and reinforcing the habit of upholding your personal boundaries is to keep track of what you did and how you felt about it.

Take a few minutes at the end of each day to note each time you acted in integrity with a personal boundary and how you felt about it.

Use this format:

Date:

What I Did:

How I Felt:

As you continue to work on strengthening your personal boundaries, they get easier to uphold each time you use them. You'll find yourself feeling stronger and less fearful more often.

The Litany of Love

I saved the best for last.

This simple exercise shifts your energy and emotions from lower-based vibrations, such as fear, depression, and anger to higher frequencies such as gratitude, appreciation, and peace.

It goes like this: whenever you're feeling an emotion or energy you don't like, you can instantly shift it to a higher, better feeling emotion or energy. You simply look around you and find things you like. It doesn't have to be all big, important things that you just adore. Even small things that you like just a little bit work. You just think a thought about how you like that thing. And then find another. And another. You keep going until you can feel that your emotion/energy has become uplifted sufficiently for you.

Practicing the Litany of Love each morning before you get out of bed sets your energy for the day to a much higher vibration. It's similar to doing aerobic exercise which sets your metabolic rate for the day.

Every morning as I wake up I begin listing all the things I love. It might go like this: "I love my purple flannel sheets. I love my warm, cozy bed. I love that picture on my wall over there. I love the smell of my essential oils. I love my cats all curled up next to

96

me. I love that I get to go to Tai Chi tonight. I love...." well, you get the picture.

As you go through your Litany of Love, you can actually feel your energy shifting upward. At some point, you'll feel a shift into joy, happiness, excitement, or some other really good-feeling emotion.

What you'll notice after practicing the Litany of Love regularly for a while is that you're just generally a happier person. And as you're being happier, you're attracting happier people, events, and things to yourself.

The Litany of Love. It's one of the many ways to enjoy the Law of Attraction in action. Try it!

The Truth

Now you can work with each of these fears and take them away one by one, using the previous exercises in this until only the truth is left standing.

And the truth is this:

You *do* deserve to have what you desire.

You *are* worthy.

You *can* have it.

Go ahead, live your life to the fullest, free from fear. It's your Divine right to joyously use your natural talents and desires to create your best life. As you do so, you'll also find how easy and wonderful it is to be of the highest and greatest service to others.

Kathy Wilson, CPC

Kathy Wilson is a Certified Professional Coach whose inner journey has meandered down many diverse paths, each one offering vast riches in the wisdom gleaned from all her life experiences. Some of these experiences include working as a pea tester, bartender, motel maid, clam digger, logger, construction superintendent, roofing contractor, Realtor, landscaper, snowmobile clothing manufacturer, and website designer.

She is the author of numerous books, all of which are available on Amazon.com in paperback and in Kindle ebook format.

Visit her website for coaching, mentoring, and teaching services she offers as well as products such as guided meditations and online courses.

www.Warrior-Priestess.com

26639574R00055

Made in the USA
Columbia, SC
14 September 2018